LEONARD BERNSTEIN
COMPLETE ANNIVERSARIES
FOR PIANO

The Name and Likeness of "Leonard Bernstein" is a registered trademark of Amberson Holdings LLC.
Used by Permission.

ISBN 978-1-4803-9358-5

LEONARD
BERNSTEIN
Music Publishing
Company LLC

BOOSEY & HAWKES

AN IMAGEM COMPANY

DISTRIBUTED BY

HAL•LEONARD®
CORPORATION
7777 W. BLUEMOUND RD. P.O. BOX 13819 MILWAUKEE, WI 53213

www.leonardbernstein.com
www.boosey.com
www.halleonard.com

LEONARD BERNSTEIN
August 25, 1918 – October 14, 1990

Leonard Bernstein was born in Lawrence, Massachusetts. He took piano lessons as a boy and attended the Garrison and Boston Latin Schools. At Harvard University he studied with Walter Piston, Edward Burlingame-Hill, and A. Tillman Merritt, among others. Before graduating in 1939 he made an unofficial conducting debut with his own incidental music to *The Birds*, and directed and performed in Marc Blitzstein's *The Cradle Will Rock*. Subsequently, at the Curtis Institute of Music in Philadelphia, he studied piano with Isabella Vengerova, conducting with Fritz Reiner, and orchestration with Randall Thompson.

In 1940 he studied at the Boston Symphony Orchestra's newly created summer institute, Tanglewood, with the orchestra's conductor, Serge Koussevitzky. Bernstein later became Koussevitzky's conducting assistant.

Bernstein was appointed to his first permanent conducting post in 1943, as Assistant Conductor of the New York Philharmonic. On November 14, 1943, Bernstein substituted on a few hours notice for the ailing Bruno Walter at a Carnegie Hall concert, which was broadcast nationally on radio, receiving critical acclaim. Soon orchestras worldwide sought him out as a guest conductor.

In 1945 he was appointed Music Director of the New York City Symphony Orchestra, a post he held until 1947. After Serge Koussevitzky died in 1951, Bernstein headed the orchestral and conducting departments at Tanglewood, teaching there for many years. In 1951 he married the Chilean actress and pianist, Felicia Montealegre. He was also visiting music professor, and head of the Creative Arts Festivals at Brandeis University in the early 1950s.

Bernstein became Music Director of the New York Philharmonic in 1958. From then until 1969 he led more concerts with the orchestra than any previous conductor. He subsequently held the lifetime title of Laureate Conductor, making frequent guest appearances with the orchestra. Over half of Bernstein's more than 400 recordings were made with the New York Philharmonic.

Bernstein traveled the world as a conductor. Immediately after World War II, in 1946, he conducted in London and at the International Music Festival in Prague. In 1947 he conducted in Tel Aviv, beginning a relationship with Israel that lasted until his death. In 1953, Bernstein was the first American to conduct opera at the Teatro alla Scala in Milan in Cherubini's *Medea* with Maria Callas.

Bernstein was a leading advocate of American composers, particularly Aaron Copland. The two remained close friends for life. As a young pianist, Bernstein performed Copland's *Piano Variations* so often he considered the composition his trademark. Bernstein programmed and recorded nearly all of the Copland orchestral works — many of them twice. He devoted several televised *Young People's Concerts* to Copland, and gave the premiere of Copland's *Connotations*, commissioned for the opening of Philharmonic Hall (now Avery Fisher Hall) at Lincoln Center in 1962.

While Bernstein's conducting repertoire encompassed the standard literature, he may be best remembered for his performances and recordings of Haydn, Beethoven, Brahms, Schumann, Sibelius and Mahler. Particularly notable were his performances of the Mahler symphonies with the New York Philharmonic in the 1960s, sparking a renewed interest in the works of Mahler.

Inspired by his Jewish heritage, Bernstein completed his first large-scale work as a composer, Symphony No. 1: "Jeremiah" (1943). The piece was first performed with the Pittsburgh Symphony Orchestra in 1944, conducted by the composer, and received the New York Music Critics' Award. Koussevitzky premiered Bernstein's Symphony No. 2: "The Age of Anxiety" with the Boston Symphony Orchestra, with Bernstein as piano soloist. His Symphony No. 3: "Kaddish," composed in 1963, was premiered by the Israel Philharmonic Orchestra. "Kaddish" is dedicated "To the Beloved Memory of John F. Kennedy."

Other major compositions by Bernstein include *Prelude, Fugue and Riffs* for solo clarinet and jazz ensemble (1949); *Serenade* for violin, strings and percussion (1954); *Symphonic Dances from West Side Story* (1960); *Chichester Psalms* for chorus, boy soprano and orchestra (1965); *Mass: A Theater Piece for Singers, Players and Dancers*, commissioned for the opening of the John F. Kennedy Center for the Performing Arts in Washington, DC, and first produced there in 1971; *Songfest*, a song cycle for six singers and orchestra (1977); *Divertimento*, for orchestra (1980); *Halil*, for solo flute and small orchestra (1981); *Touches*, for solo piano (1981); *Missa Brevis* for singers and percussion (1988); *Thirteen Anniversaries* for solo piano (1988); *Concerto for Orchestra: Jubilee Games* (1989); and *Arias and Barcarolles* for two singers and piano duet (1988).

Bernstein also wrote a one-act opera, *Trouble in Tahiti*, in 1952, and its sequel *A Quiet Place* in 1983. He collaborated with choreographer Jerome Robbins on three major ballets: *Fancy Free* (1944) and *Facsimile* (1946) for the American Ballet theater; and *Dybbuk* (1975) for the New York City Ballet. He composed the score for the award-winning movie *On the Waterfront* (1954) and incidental music for two Broadway plays: *Peter Pan* (1950) and *The Lark* (1955).

Bernstein contributed substantially to the Broadway musical stage. He collaborated with Betty Comden and Adolph Green on *On The Town* (1944) and *Wonderful Town* (1953). In collaboration with Richard Wilbur and Lillian Hellman and others he wrote *Candide* (1956). Other versions of *Candide* were written in association with Hugh Wheeler, Stephen Sondheim, et al. In 1957 he again collaborated with Jerome Robbins, Stephen Sondheim, and Arthur Laurents, on the landmark musical *West Side Story*, also made into the Academy Award-winning film. In 1976 Bernstein and Alan Jay Lerner wrote *1600 Pennsylvania Avenue*.

Festivals of Bernstein's music have been produced throughout the world. In 1978 the Israel Philharmonic sponsored a festival commemorating his years of dedication to Israel. The Israel Philharmonic also bestowed on him the lifetime title of Laureate Conductor in 1988. In 1986 the London Symphony Orchestra and the Barbican Centre produced a Bernstein Festival. The London Symphony Orchestra in 1987 named him Honorary President. In 1989 the city of Bonn presented a Beethoven/Bernstein Festival.

In 1985 the National Academy of Recording Arts and Sciences honored Mr. Bernstein with the Lifetime Achievement Grammy Award. He won eleven Emmy Awards in his career. His televised concert and lecture series started with the *Omnibus* program in 1954, followed by the extraordinary *Young People's Concerts with the New York Philharmonic* in 1958 that extended over fourteen seasons. Among his many appearances on the PBS series *Great Performances* was the acclaimed eleven-part "Bernstein's Beethoven." In 1989, Bernstein and others commemorated the 1939 invasion of Poland in a worldwide telecast from Warsaw.

Bernstein's writings were published in *The Joy of Music* (1959), *Leonard Bernstein's Young People's Concerts* (1961), *The Infinite Variety of Music* (1966), and *Findings* (1982). Each has been widely translated. He gave six lectures at Harvard University in 1972-1973 as the Charles Eliot Norton Professor of Poetry. These lectures were subsequently published and televised as *The Unanswered Question*.

Bernstein always rejoiced in opportunities to teach young musicians. His master classes at Tanglewood were famous. He was instrumental in founding the Los Angeles Philharmonic Institute in 1982. He helped create a world class training orchestra at the Schleswig Holstein Music Festival. He founded the Pacific Music Festival in Sapporo, Japan. Modeled after Tanglewood, this international festival was the first of its kind in Asia and continues to this day.

Bernstein received many honors. He was elected in 1981 to the American Academy of Arts and Letters, which gave him a Gold Medal. The National Fellowship Award in 1985 applauded his life-long support of humanitarian causes. He received the MacDowell Colony's Gold Medal; medals from the Beethoven Society and the Mahler Gesellschaft; the Handel Medallion, New York City's highest honor for the arts; a Tony award (1969) for Distinguished Achievement in the Theater; and dozens of honorary degrees and awards from colleges and universities. He was presented ceremonial keys to the cities of Oslo, Vienna, Bersheeva and the village of Bernstein, Austria, among others. National honors came from Italy, Israel, Mexico, Denmark, Germany (the Great Merit Cross), and France (Chevalier, Officer and Commandeur of the Legion d'Honneur). He received the Kennedy Center Honors in 1980.

World peace was a particular concern of Bernstein. Speaking at Johns Hopkins University in 1980 and the Cathedral of St. John the Divine in New York in 1983, he described his vision of global harmony. His "Journey for Peace" tour to Athens and Hiroshima with the European Community Orchestra in 1985, commemorated the 40th anniversary of the atom bomb. In December 1989 Bernstein conducted the historic "Berlin Celebration Concerts" on both sides of the Berlin Wall, as it was being dismantled. The concerts were unprecedented gestures of cooperation, the musicians representing the former East Germany, West Germany, and the four powers that had partitioned Berlin after World War II.

Bernstein supported Amnesty International from its inception. To benefit the effort in 1987, he established the Felicia Montealegre Fund in memory of his wife who died in 1978.

In 1990 Bernstein received the Praemium Imperiale, an international prize created in 1988 by the Japan Arts Association and awarded for lifetime achievement in the arts. Bernstein used the $100,000 prize to establish initiatives in the arts and education, principally the Leonard Bernstein Center for Artful Learning.

Bernstein was the father of three children — Jamie, Alexander, and Nina — and the grandfather of two: Francisca and Evan.

COMPLETE ANNIVERSARIES FOR PIANO

Listed chronologically by composition

SEVEN ANNIVERSARIES

Composed in Boston and New York City, 1942–43.
First performance: WNYC radio, 1943, Leonard Bernstein, piano.
First concert performance: Leonard Bernstein, piano on 14 May 1944 at the
Opera House, Boston, Massachusetts.
Duration: ca. 6 minutes.

FOUR ANNIVERSARIES

Composed in 1948. First performance: Eudice Podis, piano, on 1 October 1948;
Cleveland, Ohio.
Duration: ca. 6 minutes.

FIVE ANNIVERSARIES

Composed 1949–51. Duration: ca. 7 minutes.

THIRTEEN ANNIVERSARIES

Composition was completed in 1988. Duration: ca. 23 minutes.

The source for the historical information in this section was
Leonard Bernstein: A Complete Catalog of His Works,
Volume 1: Life, Musical Compositions & Writings
Edited by Jack Gottlieb
Published by Leonard Bernstein Music Publishing Company, LLC.

CONTENTS

FOUR ANNIVERSARIES

2   For Felicia Montealegre
4   For Johnny Mehegan
6   For David Diamond
8   For Helen Coates

FIVE ANNIVERSARIES

12   For Elizabeth Rudolf
15   For Lukas Foss
18   For Elizabeth B. Ehrman
20   For Sandy Gellhorn
22   For Susanna Kyle

SEVEN ANNIVERSARIES

24   For Aaron Copland
25   For My Sister, Shirley
26   In Memoriam: Alfred Eisner
28   For Paul Bowles
29   In Memoriam: Nathalie Koussevitzky
30   For Sergei Koussevitzky
31   For William Schuman

THIRTEEN ANNIVERSARIES

33   For Shirley Gabis Rhoads Perle
34   In Memoriam: William Kapell
35   For Stephen Sondheim
36   For Craig Urquhart
37   For Leo Smit
38   For My Daughter, Nina
40   In Memoriam: Helen Coates
42   In Memoriam: Goddard Lieberson
43   For Jessica Fleischmann
45   In Memoriam: Constance Hope
47   For Felicia, On Our 28th Birthday (& Her 52nd)
48   For Aaron Stern
50   In Memoriam: Ellen Goetz

FOUR ANNIVERSARIES

LEONARD BERNSTEIN
(1948)

I. For Felicia Montealegre
(Feb. 6, 1922)

II. For Johnny Mehegan
(June 6, 1920)

III. For David Diamond
(July 9, 1915)

Poco più mosso

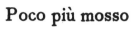

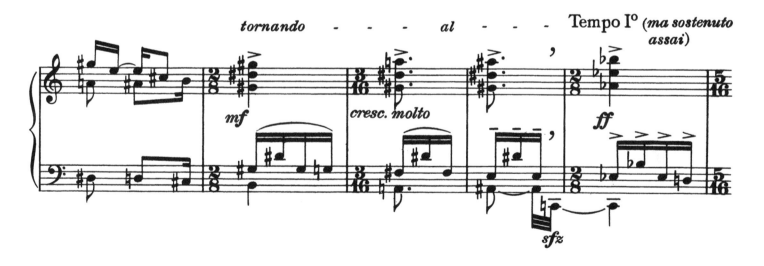

IV. For Helen Coates
(July 19, 1899)

Leonard Bernstein®

This page intentionally left blank to facilitate page turns.

FIVE ANNIVERSARIES

LEONARD BERNSTEIN
(1949–51)

I. For Elizabeth Rudolf
(born Jan. 23, 1894)

II. For Lukas Foss
(born Aug. 15, 1922)

Allegro con anima ♩= 132

III. For Elizabeth B. Ehrman
(born Jan. 22, 1883)

IV. For Sandy Gellhorn
(born April 23, 1951)

V. For Susanna Kyle
(born July 24, 1949)

Leonard Bernstein®

SEVEN ANNIVERSARIES

LEONARD BERNSTEIN
(1943)

I. For Aaron Copland
(Nov. 14, 1900)

II. For My Sister, Shirley
(Oct. 3, 1923)

III. In Memoriam: Alfred Eisner
(Jan. 4, 1941)

Andante serioso, un poco rubato (♪ = 50)

IV. For Paul Bowles

(Dec. 31, 1910)

Moderato, senza calore ($\bullet$ = 104)

p legato, subdued, the whole piece una corda

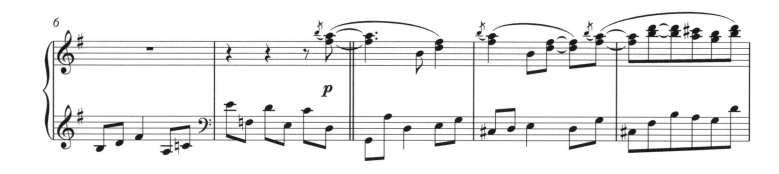

prettily

pp subito staccato

V. In Memoriam: Nathalie Koussevitzky
(Jan. 15, 1942)

VI. For Sergei Koussevitzky
(July 26, 1874)

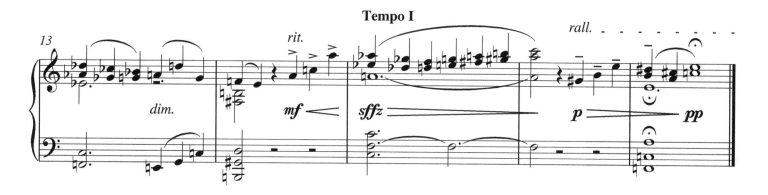

VII. For William Schuman
(Aug. 4, 1910)

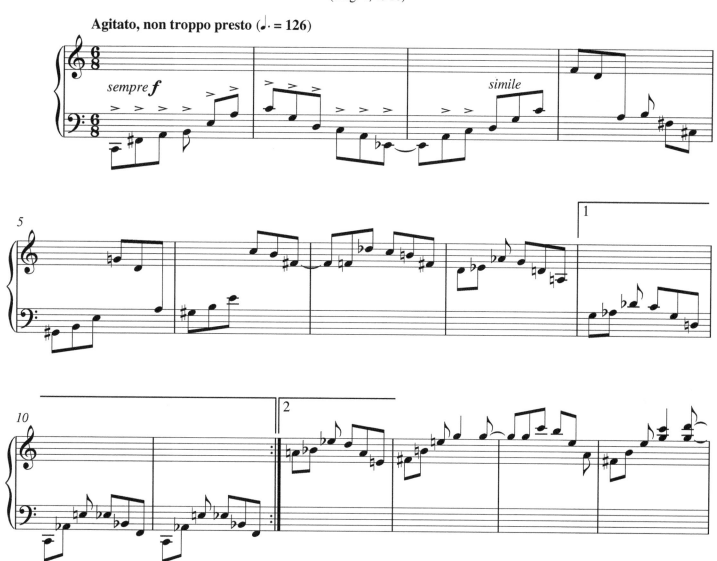

Più mosso

Boston - New York City
1942–43

THIRTEEN ANNIVERSARIES

LEONARD BERNSTEIN
(1988)

I. For Shirley Gabis Rhoads Perle

(b. April 7, 1924)

July 1981

II. In Memoriam: William Kapell

(September 20, 1922–October 29, 1953)

19 July 1981

III. For Stephen Sondheim
(b. March 22, 1930)

20 March 1965

IV. For Craig Urquhart
(b. September 3, 1953)

1960's/revised 25 November 1986

V. For Leo Smit

(b. January 12, 1921)

5 February 1988

VI. For My Daughter, Nina

(b. February 28, 1962)

January 1986

VII. In Memoriam: Helen Coates

(July 19, 1899–February 27, 1989)

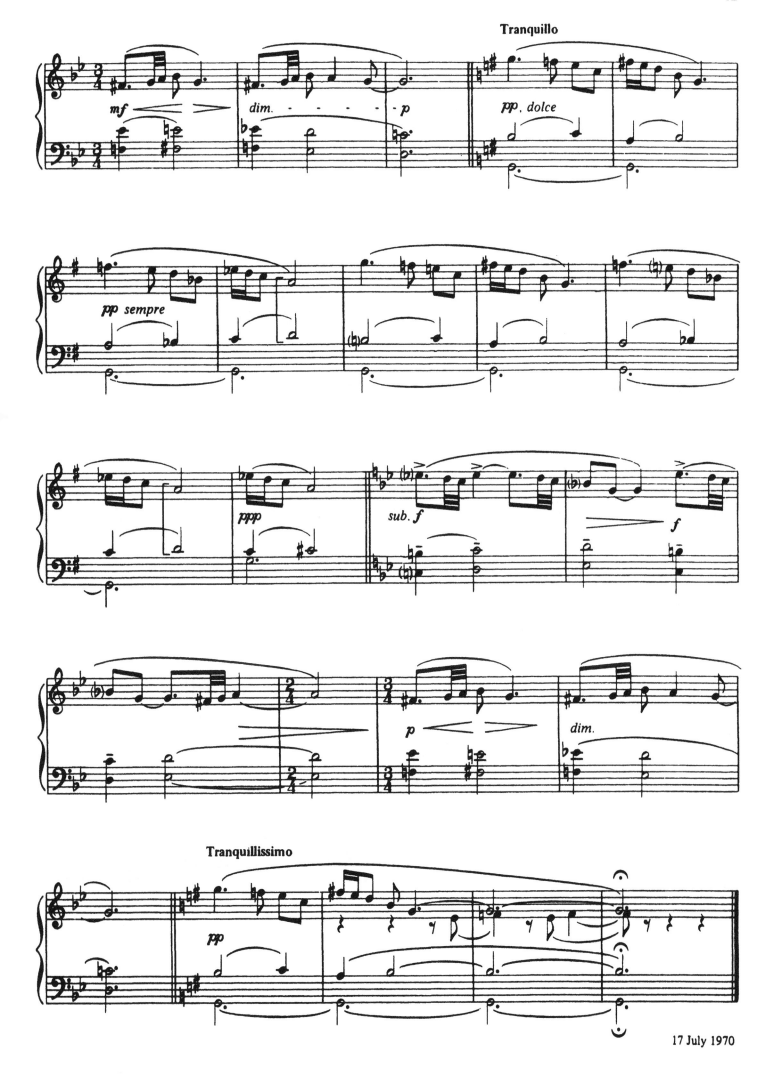

17 July 1970

VIII. In Memoriam: Goddard Lieberson

(April 5, 1911–May 29, 1977)

20 December 1964

IX. For Jessica Fleischmann
(b. September 19, 1965)

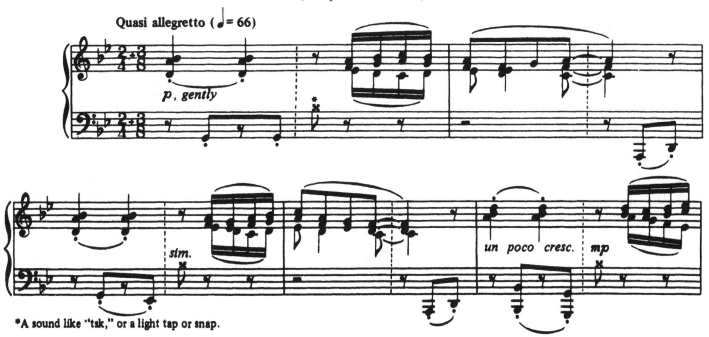

*A sound like "tsk," or a light tap or snap.

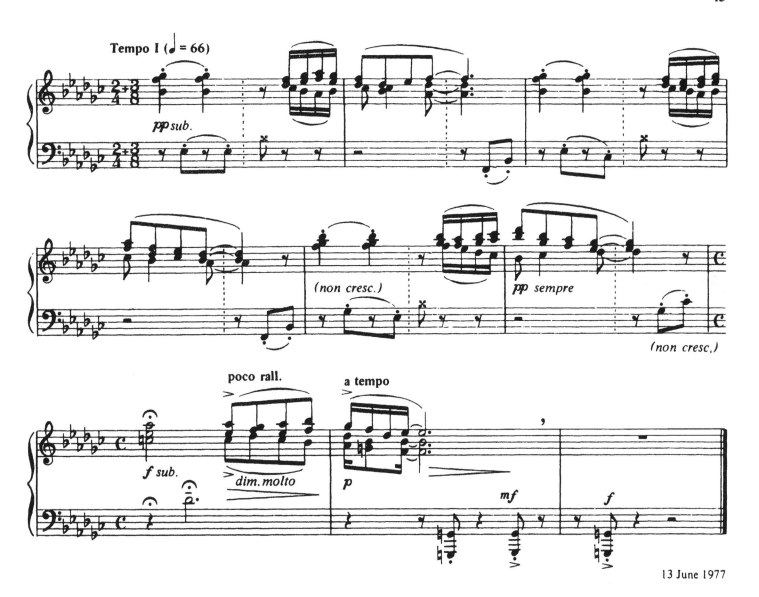

13 June 1977

X. In Memoriam: Constance Hope
(December 23, 1904–June 13, 1977)

46

poco accel. *breve* **Senza misura, rubato**
("A · las, with me the light of love is o'er...")*

f sub. (come un recitativo)

a tempo, ma un po' più lento che prima

(rall.)

Adagio, senza misura
("...No more shall bloom the thun-der blast - ed tree... No more...")*

pp, from very far

*Edgar Allen Poe: "To One in Paradise"

21 October 1977

XI. For Felicia, On Our 28th Birthday (& Her 52nd)
(February 6, 1974)*

*On this date, in 1946, Mr. Bernstein first met his future wife.

6 February 1974

XII. For Aaron Stern
(b. November 3, 1949)

15 November 1986

XIII. In Memoriam: Ellen Goetz

(June 16, 1930–January 27, 1986)

March 1986